BEYOND SUPERNATURAL REALISM

Jesus and the Call to Authenticity

Robert High Baker, PhD

ARCHWAY PUBLISHING

Archway Publishing books may be ordered
through booksellers or by contacting:

Archway Publishing
1663 Liberty Drive
Bloomington, IN 47403
www.archwaypublishing.com
1 (888) 242-5904

ISBN: 978-1-4808-5916-6 (sc)
ISBN: 978-1-4808-5917-3 (e)

Library of Congress Control Number: 2018901896

Print information available on the last page.

Archway Publishing rev. date: 02/16/2018

In memory of Marcus Borg,
a good and faithful servant.

Write what you have to, not what you ought.
—Henry D. Thoreau, *Walden*

CONTENTS

PREFACE

Like millions of Christians over the past twenty centuries, I have been profoundly influenced by the words and actions of Jesus of Nazareth as described in the New Testament Gospels. Jesus's parables about compassion, forgiveness, justice, and peace, as well as his willingness to defy authorities even at the cost of his own life, present for us our potential to live and act humanely. Jesus told his followers that his message was that of their father in heaven, the God of their fathers—but the message itself was about them, about how humans are to live. His reference to God is fully reflexive in its meaning, because it has no meaning extraneous to human life. How is it that for Jesus, and for us in the millennia to follow, "God talk" makes sense only in terms of human life? What do we mean by God, and can anything we say about God be separated from humanity?

The Easter story, the accounts of Jesus's return to his followers following his death, brought in an additional element: an experience of events that could not be explained by natural causes and were therefore believed to be of supernatural origin. Soon thereafter, the post-resurrection Jesus and the pre-resurrection Jesus were proclaimed to be one and the same, and of supernatural origin. Jesus was therefore identified with the supernatural reality that both Hebrews and Greeks assumed to exist. This ultimate reality was described differently by these two cultural traditions, but its existence was affirmed by those who henceforth proclaimed themselves as followers of the Christ, who was then identified as fully partaking of this supernatural reality. Christians ever since have been asked to accept this as fundamental to their faith.

But what if the existence of a supernatural reality no longer makes sense for us? What, if anything, does it have to do with the Jesus of the Gospels? If the God who is referenced by Jesus makes sense to us only in terms of our human existence, do we still need to understand God as a supernatural reality, or is there another way to speak of God? The discourse to follow seeks to address these questions.

1

THE CULTURAL SETTING

Two millennia ago, a new religion burst on the scene in the Mediterranean Levant. Within only a few centuries, it had become the religion favored by the Roman Empire, and it has dominated the Western world since—in cultural hegemony, if not in the steadfast faithfulness of its nominal adherents. If one seeks an explanation for this rapid development of Christianity, one might start at the physical location of its origins. The Roman province of Palestine happened to be where two powerful cultural traditions converged: the Hebraic and the Hellenistic. These two traditions, played out in the push and pull of the rationale and practices of early Christians, have continued to vex Christian thinkers in the ensuing centuries, even if Christian doctrine was ostensibly settled by authority figures who laid down orthodoxy and demanded obedience.

1

In summary form, one might frame the nature of the difference between these two traditions as follows. The Hebraic tradition has a story at its core: the story of the people of Abraham. The story tells of development of their allegiance to a tribal god who led them to a new homeland and then is revealed to them, through their leaders and prophets, as the one God, the only true God, in whom they place their ultimate trust despite the trials and tribulations of their history. It is a religion of people, of place, and of a series of events across time. Included frequently in this history are encounters and interactions between God and man. It is a religious tradition grounded in historicity and cultural practices.

The Hellenistic tradition may also be traced back to historical events in regard to the Levant: the conquest of the region by Alexander the Great around 332 BC. This conquest by Greek armies was followed by political control and cultural hegemony. (Greek culture had already been firmly established in Asia Minor for centuries.) By the time the region fell under Roman control late in the pre-Christian era, Greek language and culture dominated the literate and ruling elites.

It is not the political history, however, but the Hellenic philosophic tradition that is the key element of Greek culture as regards Christian origins. It is the ideas of Plato and his student Aristotle that formed this tradition and framed the nature of the argument for the literate Christian apologists in both the early Church and in the centuries to follow.

The core of this Greek tradition was the supremacy of rational thought as the way to truth. It argues that reason and especially abstract thought—as in mathematical reasoning and the contemplation of an abstract forms or ideas—is more valid, or "true," than sensory experience. This idea, as developed by Plato and the later Platonists who followed his ideas, argues that what is truly real are only these abstractions, and that sensory experience is thus an inferior means of knowing. This elevation of abstraction led to a dramatically new way to understand the world and underlies the development of science and, ultimately, our modern, technology-based civilization. It also has had profound implications in the development of Christianity.

Both the Hebraic and the Hellenistic traditions share a common element: belief in a supernatural reality which exists outside of human experience but which is the source of all that exists and in which ultimate truth resides. For the Hebrews, this supernatural reality was called God. God resided "up there" in heaven, wherever that heaven was, but it was not on earth. This God interacted with men, but God was something else entirely from man. For the Platonists, this supernatural reality was also an "other." Because men could imagine ideal forms, both of substance and of spirit, the Platonists argued that the true home of such ideals lay in a realm beyond the natural world. In both traditions, humans have the capacity to access this supernatural reality, but this accessibility is limited by the human condition. Nevertheless, for both the ancient Greeks and the Hebrews, supernatural reality was a given.

For modern, educated man, a concept such as a supernatural realty has virtually no relationship to his daily existence. Modern man lives in a world dominated by the science and technology that has created his world. A notion such as a supernatural reality may exist for him simply as a quaint abstraction, but it has no relationship to his life in commerce, in factory or in field, or even in the classroom.

This broad assertion is also largely true for modern, educated Christians, although they may object to the charge. The fact is that educated Christians rarely concern themselves with the notion of a supernatural reality in their daily lives. They share the same science and technology as other moderns, and they operate within this same environment. They too are inheritors of modernity.

Yet there is an exception to this generalization as applied to Christians. When the great majority of Christians address the nature of their faith and the belief system underlying that faith, they readily accept, even proclaim, the existence of a supernatural reality as the foundation of that faith. A concept fully alien to their contemporary world is embraced as central to their religion. Why?

The quite obvious reason is that this is what they have been taught to believe. The twin traditions underlying the development of Christianity were cemented into a difficult union in a statement of orthodox belief at the Council of Nicaea, early in the development of Christianity. Over the centuries, one or the other of the core elements of either the Hebraic or Platonist traditions has gained more or less traction at different times, in different places, and among the various members of the Church Universal. However, one common element has been retained: acceptance of a supernatural reality as the basis for the Christian worldview.

But need it be a given for us, as twenty-first-century Christians? Are we to be always tethered to the convictions of the ancients when so much of the cosmology of their worldview has been supplanted by centuries of discovery? Why must the vast majority of Christians today, even those who readily set aside literalist understandings of Scripture and abhor fundamentalism, still readily acknowledge the existence of a supernatural reality, considering it as an essential element of their faith? This "reality" may never enter their minds in the course of their daily lives, yet when questions of Christian belief and faith are considered, supernatural reality is the go-to place on which to rest one's convictions.

Because Christians continue to be told that they have to accept supernatural reality as central to their faith, they are loath to abandon it. But abandon it we must. The concept of a supernatural reality has led Christianity to false conclusions, false hopes, and false purposes. It has done this for centuries, but it has become a dire issue in the modern age because it has made Christianity meaningless, unworkable, and unacceptable for millions of people, specifically the educated masses on all continents, and especially for the young. Although the Christian religion retains a good bit of its former sway in the United States, it is fast losing ground there even as it has all but given up the ghost in Western Europe.

There is another way. As I shall argue, the existentialist philosophers of the past two centuries have given us an alternative way to understand what we mean by God, the nature of faith, and the power of the Christ. Existentialist thought gives us the power to let go of the limitations inherent in our cultural traditions and unveil what is essential to us as human beings. We don't need to abandon our traditions, but we do need to let go of ideas that we can't believe anymore and recognize what is true now and has always been true.

2

THE ROOTS OF ORTHODOXY

Let us first take up how these two ancient traditions develop in Christianity, specifically to look at the concept of a supernatural reality as a core element in Christianity, and the interplay between the Hebraic and Hellenistic interpretations of such a reality.

Within the Synoptic Gospels, which scholars believe were written in the second half of the first century to the early second century, we find recollections about the activities and ministry of the pre-Resurrection Jesus and the post-Resurrection Jesus. As recorded in the Gospels, Jesus often refers to his "father in heaven" and other such references to a reality that is beyond that of normal earthly existence—a reality that is supernatural in that it is outside normal experience even thought it interacts with earthly experience. This concept is fully part and parcel of the Hebraic tradition, and indeed of ancient cultures in general. It precedes and exists alongside any developments in Greek philosophy, and it is part of a generally accepted understanding of reality across cultures in that period (and indeed for millions of people in ours as well.)

The Synoptic Gospels also include accounts of Jesus's ultimate transition to a spiritual reality beyond his earthly reality. These include the transfiguration story, in which Jesus is seen by some of his disciples as appearing in heaven alongside the Hebrew prophet Elijah and the Hebrew leader Moses. They include scenes after Jesus's death, where he appears as an angel, and also his appearance to his followers when he allows himself to be revealed. There is also the ascension story, in which Jesus is finally taken up into heaven.

While referring to a supernatural reality, these events are portrayed as encounters within history, as are the stories about the resurrected Jesus who eats and drinks with his followers. His disciples in Jerusalem, including Peter and Jesus's brother, James, were his followers before his crucifixion, were included among those to whom the "resurrected" Jesus appeared, and who became leaders of the early Christian community there. The presumption of the Gospels is that it is their witness, and others', that is the basis for the events recorded.

Thus, the Synoptic Gospels draw from the prevailing cultural Hebraic tradition, as well as that of other extant cultural traditions in the Mediterranean and in Asia, in their assumption that there exists a supernatural reality that may at times interact with human affairs. In that the Gospels are themselves put forth as history about real people and events in specific places and time, they also are very much in the mode of the Hebraic tradition.

It is in the earliest writings in the Christian canon, the authentic letters of the Apostle Paul of Tarsus, that we see the Hellenistic tradition emerge in Christian thinking. In his letters to the Christian communities he helped establish across the Mediterranean world, Paul contemplates the meaning of the life and death of Jesus. What is essential for Paul is not the teaching and ministry of Jesus of Nazareth as described in the Synoptic Gospels, but rather Jesus's death, the form of that death, and the Resurrection. His focus is on the Christ—the meaning of the crucified Jesus and his resurrection for Paul and for early Christians.

Resurrection, as Paul describes it in his letters, is a transformation of the human Jesus into a spiritual being, a transformed being who Paul himself encounters well after the period of the ascension. Clearly this encounter is the foundation for Paul's faith, and its reality for him is the basis for his ministry to others. In his writing, Paul references this transformed Jesus, the Christ, not simply as a human being transitioned into a supernatural entity but as spiritual reality itself. His argument uses the language of Platonic thought to describe the nature of this spiritual reality in a manner very unlike the Synoptic Gospel writers.

Paul's understanding of the nature of the transformed Jesus is not fully and consistently developed in his letters, but the language of his contemplation on the nature of the Christ and Christ's relationship to believers had a profound impact on the development of Christian thought. Is Paul's Christ a purely spiritual reality in the nature of a Platonic spiritual reality? If this is the "truly real," does that mean that Jesus only appeared human but was in reality something else? Is the Godhead knowable only as an abstraction, or can it be accessed by means other than thought? What does Paul mean when he says that Christ "revealed himself to me"? Is a thought statement, a statement of about Christ or about God, a necessary aspect of faith? Each of these concerns became important, even central, in the later development of Christianity.

It would be a mistake to limit Paul and his letters to any of such arguments, because his language and imagery transcend our attempts to limit his meaning. It is important to add that Paul's account of his encounter with the risen Jesus is just that: a story of a personal encounter with this transformed Jesus, an encounter at a specific time and place—a part of his story, not simply a contemplation. His use of Platonic imagery is thus conditioned by his personal affirmation. Yet it is this very language and imagery used by Paul in discussing the meaning of the Christ that became such an important element in later Christian thought.

What is common to both the Hebraic tradition and the Hellenistic philosophical tradition is an assertion that there is a supernatural reality "out there" in some manner, a transcendent truth that may be revealed to humans by instigation of the supernatural entity or may be accessed by humans via their own faculties, especially by contemplation. The natural world and the human world may reflect this supernatural truth, but the reflection points to a reality beyond.

The Hebraic tradition's stories of encounters with this supernatural reality and the Hellenistic philosophic focus on contemplation and abstract claims about a transcendental reality each made its way into what ultimately became an uneasy meshing of the two strains together within orthodox statements of belief, most specifically in the Creed of Nicaea formulated in the fourth century CE. In the Nicene Creed, the Jesus of history is described, but he is also described in the language of philosophy as transcendent truth, preexisting any historical reality. The Christ is fully human, the Jesus of history, but is also the preexisting Godhead. The living, breathing

Jesus who was crucified and then transitions to a supernatural reality in the Gospel stories is absorbed, in the language of the Creed, into an equally transcendent reality beyond human experience, even if such a reality may be contemplated and asserted by man.

In their attempt to fuse the twin cultural traditions of the Levant, the Church fathers who sat in Nicaea mixed them together in such a manner that the Church has been wrestling with them ever since. Even the fact that the Church has historically claimed—that in order to be a faithful Christian, one must assent to the assertions within the Creed—takes a stand on one side of the dual traditions, the Hellenistic. Yet it is the stories of the teaching and ministry of the human Jesus, the "good news" as laid out in the four Gospels, that has been the principal claim upon the faith of millions of Christians across the centuries.

But what no longer seems credible for millions of educated Westerners is the concept of a supernatural reality as described either within the Creed or within the twin traditions that created it. The notion of a God "out there," either in the Hebraic sense or as a philosophical concept, is simply not part of the modern mind. And insofar as the notion of such a supernatural reality plays a role in Christian thinking, it becomes a stumbling block for moderns. But as we have seen, this has indeed been the direction toward which both traditions have pointed, both within their own development historically and when combined and fused within Christian thought.

Today, the Church continues to ask the faithful to adhere to creedal orthodoxy and think in terms of the descriptions of reality proscribed by Hebraic and Hellenistic thought. It continues to proclaim the existence of a supernatural reality in the face of the abandonment of the notion in the everyday thinking of even its own faithful adherents, even if they continue to proclaim it on Sundays. There exists a profound disconnect between the modern mind and the ancient orthodoxy of the Church.

Yet even with the chasm of separation between the modern mind and creedal orthodoxy, and despite centuries of philosophy and theology in the interim, there would appear to be aspects of the Hebraic and Hellenistic traditions that we don't want to give up. The core elements of each tradition—the story of human experience as incorporated within the Hebraic tradition, and the world-altering advance of abstract thought in the Hellenistic tradition—remain the twin poles of Western thought. Despite its awkward fusing of these traditions, the Creed seems to speak to us because it contains within its formulation something so essential about who we are and what we know. As such, it remains both intriguing and somehow relevant even as it asks us to accept what we cannot accept.

Philosophy and (in some cases) theology have moved on in myriad ways in the centuries since the Council of Nicaea. But for the most part, the Church clings to its ancient formulations, seemingly unable to forthrightly buy in to proposed reassessments. The reason for the reluctance to accept change may simply be blind adherence to its traditions, but there also may be a failure to find a rethinking of the meaning of the essential elements of Christianity that effectively responds to how modern man understands his reality. Is there a way back to what still calls to us from within the twin cultural traditions that created Christianity, a way that lets go of the notion of the supernatural but not the mystery of our existence? Is there a way that leads back to God?

3

AN EXISTENTIALIST PRIMER

hat is real? What is true? What is the nature of Jesus, and what is meant by revelation? What does the Resurrection tell us?

Is Jesus a supernatural drop-in sent to show us what the supernatural is all about, or is he fully human (and only human), and his revelation is about the nature of human existence itself? Can what we call God be a reality other than supernatural?

It is toward this end that the following discussion is addressed. The basis for the discussion is a description of man derived from thinkers deemed existentialists, and it includes writers from the late nineteenth through the mid-twentieth century. Those I will feature most prominently here are Soren Kierkegaard and Martin Heidegger. I will refer in the text to passages from *Irrational Man*, by William Barrett, a mid-twentieth-century discussion of existentialism that remains one of the most readable and knowledgeable assessments of that philosophic movement.[1]

Two principal areas of philosophic interest for the existentialists are epistemology (the study of the origin and nature of knowledge) and the conclusions that may be drawn from epistemology about man's understanding of reality. Existentialism raises the question of "What is man?" that makes him different from other things in his world. Is there something so fundamentally unique about humans that describing our human existence in the same manner as we might scientifically describe other things is inadequate? If we adequately address the nature of our existence, does it change how we live? Does it change our understanding of our relationship with other humans and the world we inhabit?

What the existentialists call human existence begins with a look at how humans know what they know. Man has a body and may be properly considered as a thing, with all that might be said about this from a scientific perspective. But the existentialist argues that the essence of our humanness is that man has a "more than" corporeal bodily reality. Our bodies interact with their environment from birth by means of our senses, creating relationships that have meaning even before we have any capacity to name such meaning, This embodied self is foundational but is not the end of it. Human existence is at once both corporeal and symbolic. Our bodies, and the natural world we inhabit, are finite and limited, but the world we create as humans encompasses much more than the corporeal. The human mind, corporeal and finite in itself, creates a world that includes, and is in fact created by, symbolic constructs that are presented in language, mathematics, and artistic objects. These constructs include such ideas as the infinite, the ideal, and all that is now known. Human existence thus contains, as an essential component, this capacity of creation, this power of imagination.

Martin Heidegger calls human existence, in German, *Dasein*." Dasein, he says, is German for "being in the world." William Barrett calls this a field theory of man. Man, as he exists, is not defined by his physical self but by his relationship, care, and concern for what lies both within and without that physical body.[2]

Heidegger calls the mode of Dasein an openness because it is a going beyond itself to create a relationship, an openness with another existent in which aspects of the other are revealed. Heidegger describes ways in which humans do this: mood, understanding, and speech. Understanding is the basis upon which the world opens before us. Something stands beyond oneself and becomes real to us. Our existence is what enables "what is" to become present (revealed) to us.[3]

Furthermore, in this process of revelation, Dasein allows the presence, the beingness of a thing, to become manifest. Human existence, therefore, is essential to both the knowledge about a thing that exists in our world and to an awareness of the presence of that thing. Yet there remains within that process of revelation both what becomes unhidden and what remains hidden, for in man's finitude, there is always something hidden.[4]

Language is fundamental in this orientation of the human being to another thing or human being. Even an unuttered sign, as in pointing with a finger, reflects this. One person can use a sign to create an understanding with another person, and this becomes a type of language. This relationship, an attunement between beings, becomes the basis for knowledge. Language, thus broadly defined, is our principal means of creating openness and is of the very essence of human existence.[5]

When Heidegger speaks of the presence of what is revealed, he seeks to recall what Barrett says is an aspect of human knowledge that has been lost, or at least unexplored, by Western philosophy from its emergence in ancient Greece. This lost knowledge is the "is-ness" of a thing, the awareness of its presence for us as opposed to its attributes. This concern with the being or presence of something became even more abandoned as an area of study by philosophers when the separation of subject and object became a special focus of epistemology for Rene Descartes, who profoundly influenced later Western thought.[6]

For Heidegger, though, the awareness of presence is profound. He speaks of this awareness of presence as a recognition of being itself, and our response to this awareness is thankfulness: to thank with gratitude for the revelation of what is hidden.[7] In his work, Heidegger speaks of how this awareness comes into consciousness when something new is revealed, as for instance, in a work of art. Something new is named, it becomes unhidden, and the ordinariness of our response to our world is broken by revelation. Heidegger describes this experience as recognition of the holy. It is our response, in gratitude, for what is. Truth lies in this process of unveiling. What becomes known is contingent, because our capacity to know is limited, but we acknowledge truth in the unveiling.

One fundamental aspect of man's openness is that it is temporal as well as spatial. Man understands the tenses of time: the as-yet past, the here and now, and the not-as-yet future. Heidegger argues that the priority for man is the not-as-yet toward which man orients himself. Man turns toward this open future, taking on the burden of the past as he projects himself forward.[8]

Implicit in both spatial and temporal openness is an

understanding of its limitations: the finitude that is part and parcel of existence. The future toward which man is projected includes death, the knowledge of non-being for any individual person. This understanding of non-being, if fully acknowledged, is that it is an immediate potential for any person at any time. It is not theoretical nonexistence. It is my ever-present sense of my own possible immediate nonexistence. The now of non-being is thus a reality that must be accepted, argues Heidegger, before one's projection toward the future can become authentic. Accepting our "radical finitude" frees us from petty concerns and enables "making our lives personally and significantly our own."[9]

In this focus on personal understanding of our ever-present possibility of non-being, Heidegger echoes earlier voices that preceded twentieth-century existentialism. Barrett points to Blaise Pascal's understanding of nothingness as an immediate possibility—a "radical contingency" as one of these precursors.[10]

Another earlier voice was Soren Kierkegaard, who described an understanding of non-being as dread, an essential aspect of knowledge that must make itself present and felt in an individual if he is to become an authentic self. Kierkegaard describes in "Fear and Trembling" the process by which an individual is able to move beyond living a conventional ethical and religious life and become authentically religious. When an individual is forced to choose between two rival ethically good actions, he encounters a recognition of his radical finitude. In making an either/or decision, an individual is faced with a "real" choice, for to make one choice is to permanently negate the other and move into an outcome yet unknown. This authentic religious truth is, for Kierkegaard, a personal approbation of truth, the "ethical and religious passion of the individual."[11]

Kierkegaard's description of the development of authenticity is echoed in Heidegger's description of man's fallenness as the state of one's seeing oneself as "the One," as one among many, simply one filling a role, as in acting according to social norms and conventional morality because "one must do this." In a state of fallenness, the individual is "spared the terror and dignity of becoming an authentic self."[12] Finding one's authentic self is thus implicit in an understanding of the nature of human existence. Authenticity, in this meaning, is much more than an individual finding his own voice as distinct from his peers. Rather, it is acknowledging what makes all humans unique among all other created beings.

In summary, the existentialists affirm the unique status of human beings. It is the starting place for their examination of what is, what is true, and what it means to be human. They claim for man a special capacity for creating the possibility of knowing, which is unique to man and which includes knowledge of the presence or being of something.

4

TRUTH AND FAITH

In recognizing this unique capacity for openness as an essential aspect of authentic human existence, one might also acknowledge that there must be a source for this creative power. But is this source some objective but unknowable reality outside of our existence, or is it both within and without us? Is what we call God inseparable from human existence itself? Is there a critical link between existentialism and religion in general? Is any such link religion-specific?

One scholar who explored these issues was John MacQuarrie in his work "An Existentialist Theology: A Comparison of Heidegger and Bultmann."[13] This work focuses on Martin Heidegger's clear influence on the theology of mid-twentieth-century Christian theologian Rudolf Bultmann. Before setting off to examine this comparison specifically, MacQuarrie first notes how the biblical understanding of man differs from the dominant philosophic approach of Western history. MacQuarrie quotes W. Eichrodt's, *Man in the Old Testament.* that in the biblical tradition "the Creator's greatest gift to man, that of a personal 'I', necessarily places him, in analogy with God's being, at a distance from nature." MacQuarrie says,

> This understanding of the being of man is far removed from Greek attempts to determine and classify his space within the unity of the cosmos, for instance, as a rational animal. It is equally far removed from the Cartesian notion of *res cogitans*, which, however distinct from *res extensa*, still remains res, an objective concept which fails to do justice to the personal "I" that is made in the image of the creator. And it is poles apart from modern endeavours to understand man scientifically, as though he were nothing but an unusually complicated phenomenon of nature.

Thus, the biblical conception aligns with "the philosophy of existence" which "does not depersonalize man, as any philosophy which objectifies him must do," continues MacQuarrie.[14]

This biblical understanding of man addresses individual responsibility before God: obedience, personal consciousness of guilt, and a call for decision. MacQuarrie writes,

> These are remarkably similar to the main themes of existentialist philosophy. The responsibility of the individual confronted with

the possibility of being himself and the possibility of losing himself, fallenness, guiltiness,
resolve, temporality, death—these are prom-
inent among the phenomena which such a
philosopher as Heidegger considers to be
constitutive structures of the being of man.[15]

To describe these similarities regarding man is not to say
that the existentialist description of man necessarily gives some
account of the being of God, says MacQuarrie. "Yet in any case
we must understand the being of God as somehow analogous
to our own, if we are to speak of him at all. The Bible certainly
does so. It thinks of God as personal and historical—'the living
God' is typical and significant expression" and is, he notes,
substantially different from the Greek/Descartian/objectivist
expression of a creator." "This concept is utterly different from
the concepts of God which have been current in Greek and
western philosophy—the Unmoved Mover, the First Cause,
the Timeless Absolute and so on. Where these concepts have
influenced theological thought, they have obscured the authentic biblical understanding of God."[16]

But if these similarities suggested by MacQuarrie between
an existentialist description of man and the biblical expression
of the nature of God and the relationship between God and
man are so strong, could it be that the biblical description of
man and God arises from an ancient, even fundamental understanding of human existence that was lost, or at least often hidden, behind centuries of philosophic theorizing and abstraction? Perhaps in its focus on the uncovering the essential nature
of the being of man, the existentialists were rediscovering what
was lost. In doing so, this existentialist effort of recovery as to
what is authentically human may also be inevitably leading to

what can be said about God. If the biblical understanding of God is indeed analogous to an accurate understanding of our humanity, can it not also be that any authentic understanding of God must necessarily arise from human experience and how that experience is understood?

Indeed, can anything we say about God be separated from human experience?

What is there then, in this understanding of what it is to be authentically human, or the re-discovery of this, that would lead us to speak of God? I would argue that it lies in our aware-ness of what authentic human existence is and its relationship to Truth. If human existence—Dasein—is our capacity to be that opening which allows Truth to become known, then it will be in this unveiling that we will find an intersection between the creator and the created in which the revelation of both man and the source of man's being are to be found.

The truth spoken of here, states MacQuarrie (and follow-ing Heidegger), is "original truth." It is "not the correspon-dence of statements to facts ... but the 'light of nature,' the disclosure of being-in-the-world to itself, which makes all un-derstanding and knowledge possible."[17] MacQuarrie says that theology—that is, statements about God—are "statements which communicate that existential knowledge to which orig-inal truth belongs." But he goes on to rather qualify this by arguing that that this "existential knowledge of God" is an insight or understanding implicit in the experience of God "in faith," and that a phenomenological theology would mean "a descriptive analysis of the self's experience of God in faith." "In religious faith," he argues, "God is disclosed immediately with the self and the world."[18]

But what if the experience of God is also given in this disclosure of our existential reality? Contrary to MacQuarrie's argument that an awareness of God is preconditioned by faith, this knowledge is rather unveiled as a fundamental element of existential disclosure. As the self and the world are disclosed, so is the reality of God disclosed—and faith is the response, rather than the basis for what is described in theology. I would argue that it is out of this experience of disclosure, this experience of foundational "understanding" as described by the existentialists, that religious experience also arises. If theological statements mean a description of the self's experience of God in faith, they fundamentally arise from the self's experience of God, as certainly that is what faith means. First the experience of God, then a response to this experience, followed by attempts to describe this experience. Faith, then, is no more an assent to propositional statements about God than original truth is about the correspondence of statements to facts. Faith arises, and we speak out of it about God and our experience of God.

Despite arguing that it is faith that preconditions knowledge of God, MacQuarrie also suggests that it is this unveiling of God that actually preconditions faith when he writes that religious awe is realized in "God's revelation of himself" and "that faith, as a way of being, is man's response" to this revelation.[19] This revelation of truth as the source of our experience of the world is at once a revelation of that which makes all things possible, which we call God, but also reflects back to ourselves as human beings, with all our limitations but also all our potential. It has to reflect back to ourselves because it partakes of the very essence of what we are as human. This realization, suggests MacQuarrie, provides man with an innate understanding of God that is "given with man's understanding of his own existence" and arises from "the very constitution of man's being."[20]

MacQuarrie goes on to relate religious awe to what Rudolf Otto speaks to in "The Idea of the Holy," which MacQuarrie describes as a phenomenological study of "man's experience of the Holy." Following Otto's description of this awe, "the divine being is experienced as wholly other" that has historically been described using symbolical and mythical language. This "Ground of Being" is recognized not as a cause in any scientific sense. It is the creative element of God, disclosed in the "mysterium," and is spoken of only by analogy as a ground or cause.[21]

Religious awe is often experienced as uncanny, mystical, or otherworldly even though it is fully grounded in man's existence. This feeling comes to us, perhaps, because in our normal living, we lose sight of ourselves as special, existential, being-in-the-world, and it is only when we escape everyday facticity that we can sense this awe. Those who have experienced spiritual awe have often gone on to see themselves as alien in the so-called normal world. The "normal" way of living permits us to too easily forget what makes humans exceptional. To have an experience in which we confront our authentic self is abnormal because we too often live in a state of fallenness.

5

EXISTENTIAL THEMES IN CHRISTIANITY

What, then, can we say about God based on this existential understanding of man's authentic self? First, God is for us as a reality of lived experience, but not as an object within the created world, and neither is it outside of our experience of that world. Religious experience, and our response in faith, thus arises from our deepest understanding of what it means to be human. Heidegger and other existential thinkers, by means of their phenomenological descriptions of human experience, have helped us to rediscover essential aspects of human existence, which includes this experience of the holy. I want to emphasize *rediscover*, because much of Western culture has pushed us to suppress this knowledge. The varieties of religious experience in human history, biblical and otherwise, have nevertheless described man's experience of the sacred.

As noted earlier, Heidegger described the thankfulness that is expressed by an acknowledgment of the truth (by which the presence of what is becomes unveiled) as an experience of the holy. It is an experience of the sacred and is, in the fullest sense, a spiritual experience. Original truth—Truth with a capital T—is shown to be not a propositional statement but rather a foundational reality, a reflection of a fundamental aspect of human existence. In an acknowledgment of our existential reality, we are enabled to see other people and the natural and the inherited man-made world as fully present to us, as a gift. Thankfulness is our response to this gift.

As regards Martin Heidegger's religiosity, or lack thereof, scholars have noted that his philosophy was "essentially religious" in that its quest for being seems to be a seeking for God. But it does not achieve the end of such a quest, perhaps because for Heidegger, an existential knowledge of God had "been overlaid, trivialized, and stratified by the dead hand of tradition and dogmatism."[22]

In his ongoing effort to avoid the danger of treating man as an object rather than as Dasein, Heidegger focused on exploring man's intimacy with his natural environment and on the language and culture that emerged from this intimacy. His area of concern, especially in his later years, became the small world of rural Germany in which he lived. Unfortunately, in so narrowing his focus, Heidegger became victimized—perhaps self-victimized—by the perversion of this in the ethnocentric worship of the "Volk" in the worldview of the National Socialists. Heidegger failed to see where these impulses were leading under the Nazis, and he acquiesced to their political ambitions, or at the least refused to speak against them. There is, however, nothing in Heidegger's description of existential authenticity that would cause one to eschew an opportunity to treat all others with compassion and respect. Instead, living authentically should enable those opportunities.

The ramifications of the experience of the sacred are many. One such aspect is that it speaks to something that transcends our corporeal existence and the corporeality of the created world. It is beyond beings and aspects of beings, such as existing in space and time. As such, it speaks of the eternal. It is the great "I Am" in the face of nothingness. It is the eternal creative essence that gives being to all beings. When we fail to acknowledge this, we may easily lose sight of our true self and the true source of what makes humans fundamentally different from all other beings. That is the primary sin in biblical terms. It leads one to worship the created rather than the creator: building one's life on the world and not on God. It is losing one's self in the world by surrendering one's true self.

MacQuarrie notes that the Genesis story is about just this: the disclosure of the created world and of the self. The world is made available for me, but it is a world in which I might lose myself by loving it more than the creator.[23] Indeed, that would seem to be the essential nature of man's Fall in biblical terms. The balance of the Old Testament is the story of men and women, the people of Israel, losing their true selves and being called again and again to repent and recover their true being.

Let us look now at how the biblical tradition might be reframed in this existential way of thinking about our humanity, the nature of truth, what is real, the nature of God, and what this means specifically for Christians.

Take the core themes of Judeo-Christianity: exile and return, slavery and freedom, being lost and then reunited, death and rebirth. Might not these be seen as metaphorical descriptions of the truth of our existence? Our openness in the world makes truth possible, but our individual truth is limited by our finitude. The circumstances of our existence provide that we carry our past into the here and now and project into the future. We are what has been, is now, and what can be. But it is to the future that we are open and that gives us the possibility of hope, freedom, discovery, and transformation—even the radical transformation of being reborn into a new life of the spirit. And it is the ever-flowing gift of our existence that makes this possible.

Resurrection is rebirth, a future that is constantly being renewed, a world constantly coming into being for us, an unending wellspring that we can understand as such only when we have internalized our own non-being and the nothingness that stands in counterpoint to all that becomes present to us. To live in the spirit is to accept and to give thanks for this life-sustaining presence transcending our personal, finite existence, but that becomes accessible to us only because of the very nature of human existence. This response is our recognition and gratefulness for the eternal, creative power that underlies all being.

The spiritual impulse may be seen as our response to this understanding of our authentic existence, and the basis for finding our authentic self. When we reach our authentic self by casting ourselves beyond the customary rules of society, and move with fear and trembling into either/or choice, we acknowledge the radical finitude of our existence, becoming face-to-face with the actual possibility of our immediate nonexistence. William Barrett, in his discussion of Tolstoy's *The Death of Ivan Ilyich,* points out that it is only when Ivan comes face-to-face with the certainty of his own death, not as a theoretical possibility but as a reality, that he is able to move beyond a conventional understanding of himself into authentic understanding.[24]

Is this not the nature of a truly authentic religious existence—a concern with "ultimate things" as the source of meaning and purpose in life? Religion, seen in this way, is organizing one's life in line with what is ultimately significant. In his ministry, Jesus says again and again that we must be ready for the end, because this end is always with us and creates a call upon how we live our lives. The eschatological language employed by Jesus may be seen not only as an actual "end of the world" reality to come, but a metaphor for the reality for each of us. If we accept this reality fully, we become more truly and authentically alive.

The writer Walker Percy employs this symbolism in his novels, wherein he describes how men and women become enlivened by the sudden appearance of potential disaster, such as a hurricane. They are shaken out of the ordinariness of their lives and become more fully human, often more caring and concerned for others. The sudden intrusion of non-being as a reality penetrates the thoughtlessness by which people live out their lives. They are, in a sense, reborn into authenticity and able to live, if even for a short time, with a renewed appreciation for their own lives and life around them.

Percy also makes use of the imagery of an impending apocalypse to dramatize the awful responsibility of authentic choice in the close of his masterpiece, *The Moviegoer*. As the novel ends, the sky over New Orleans reflects the fiery flares of Mississippi River refineries as Binx Bolling commits himself to his tortured cousin Kate and to an uncertain future. The backdrop to their new life together is this unnerving, seemingly dangerous environment—a reflection, perhaps, of the potential disaster that may lie in the future, thanks to Kate's brittle psyche. But Binx makes the choice to leave his prior life of perpetual non-commitment and link his fate to Kate's, whatever that fate might hold. For Binx, this is an either/or choice. It is a religious choice.

6

JESUS AND SPIRITUAL REALITY

Let us now use the forgoing analysis and look at Jesus: his life, his works, his teaching, his death, and what this has come to mean for Christians.

Jesus was a finite, corporeal human being who lived and died in a specific time and place. Yet for Christians, he is much more than this, because he is acclaimed as the apotheosis of humans, the one who in his life, his teachings, and his death is the ideal human. And what are these ideal qualities? They are ethical. They define how human beings should live in relationship with others, and indeed within the natural environment in which they live. These qualities deal with life in this world, the world of human existence, and a world of finitude, of limits. I would posit that these ethical ideals are meaningful only in that context.

Can the Good Samaritan be compassionate if there is no pain to arouse his compassion? Can there be a need for justice if there is not a perceived finitude of resources and goods? What does peace mean outside of human conflict? Can one sacrifice oneself for another if there is no death?

Jesus's life, death, and teachings have no power outside of this world, the world of human existence, whether in 30 CE or 2017 CE. In this world, human beings are born, live, and then die. The ethical values Jesus lives out and espouses are otherworldly only in the sense that they are values of human interaction that are in opposition to the normative values of this world: the prevailing cultural values that favor self-interest over self-sacrifice, see violence as a means to settle conflict, and allow the dominant to take advantage of the weak.

The contrarian ethical values espoused by Jesus, values set in opposition to the norm, developed alongside the normative values. Across the ages, in a variety of cultures, these alternative ethical values have also been conveyed from person to person, from generation to generation, in tales, myths, and teachings. They pose an idealized value system that might theoretically exist, and in fact some propose that such an ideal reality must exist because it can be theorized. Yet such a conclusion is not necessary. It is of the very nature of human existence to symbolically conceive of perfection, but that does not presume its existence.

Jesus's sacrificial death is emblematic of his embodiment of this ethical idealism. The nature of his dying demonstrated his fully giving of himself for others, the quintessence of the sacrificial life he taught. When his followers considered as a whole the nature of his teaching, his compassion, and his sacrifice on the cross, Jesus was revealed to them as the epitome of being fully human. Those ideals transcend any one person but have meaning only in the context of human finitude, both his and ours.

To express their understanding of what this meant, the first Christians used terms such as "Son of God" and "adopted by God," because they thought in terms of a supernatural reality that lay beyond the finite, natural world that would enable Jesus to be who and what he was. But Jesus did not need to be supernatural because his ideals, his life, and the nature of his death were aspects of human existence. The ethical values he embodied were not new to Jesus. They had been a part of his own cultural tradition for centuries, and he referenced that tradition constantly in his ministry.

But wait a minute. This suggests that we should see Jesus as an ethical guide—a great one. But there are others. Why has he been considered part of the Godhead for two thousand years? There have been great teachers of wisdom through the ages, but they have not been worshiped. How does one explain the Christian religion?

I suggest that those who heard Jesus teach, minister to the infirm, and express his obvious compassion for his fellow man were moved to believe that his words and actions expressed something so profoundly true about humanity that to encounter him was to encounter the holy. His words and actions expressed something so fundamental that they transcended their time and place and seemed to emerge from truth itself. His followers proclaimed that he was "truly the son of God" because his words and actions made manifest what their historic Jewish faith had been proclaiming for thousands of years. To encounter Jesus in the first century CE was a religious experience. What he proclaimed was not just true for their own lives but for all lives, in all times. It delineated the creative force that gave their lives meaning, and it declared that this was the reality that was eternal. He offered his followers the capacity to partake of this eternal life. This is the true bread of life, he promised: to share in what is true and valuable and everlasting.

This encounter with Jesus, whether in reading the Gospels,

hearing his words proclaimed, or seeing others emulate his healing and compassionate treatment of others, has been and continues to be a religious experience. For us, these are a revelation—indeed, for many, *the* revelation—of who we are as authentically human and what we are to be about.

To be certain, other aspects of Jesus's story became central to Christians, such as the nature of his death and what it came to mean for his followers. One of these is the Christian concept of atonement. Atonement—for Christians, the reconciliation of man to God— is an adaptation of the Jewish rite of sacrificial giving to God at the temple in Jerusalem. For the ancient Jews, this sacrificial offering restored the original relationship between man and God. Their sins were forgiven, not forgotten. They were set aside so that their future selves could act responsibly and authentically. Christians came to see the crucifixion of Jesus as a summation of this sacrificial offering, in that Jesus offered up himself on behalf of others for all men and for all time. This understanding was given particular weight when the Roman destruction of the Jerusalem temple in 70 CE made the ancient Jewish rite unavailable. Thus early Christians saw this atoning death of Jesus as *the* gift of grace, a once-for-all-time act of reconciliation. (A later understanding of this concept of atonement, which sees the death of Jesus as an act of propitiation, or blood sacrifice demanded by God for the sins of men, is a pervasive perversion of this.)

This act of atonement, whether viewed in the ancient Jewish tradition or in the Christian tradition, may be seen as a gift that enables man to be restored to his authenticity. For many Christians, the atoning act of the crucifixion is what enables this restoration, but it can also be seen as a symbol of the reality that we are constantly being offered: restoration of who we truly are, if we choose to acknowledge it. The saving grace represented by the sacrifice of Jesus is a spiritual reality that is available to all men. Jesus did not give us salvation in the sense of sacrificial substitution. Rather, he showed us in his act of self-sacrifice, an act of radical devotion to truth, what salvation really means. It means giving over the self to that which is greater than the self, to the truth that is the true home of our being. The Christian name for this reality is "the love of God."

In the Gospel of John, we see the Greek cultural tradition's profound influence on the development of doctrine in the early Church, as his terminology seemed to suggest that the spiritual reality represented by the ministry, life, and death of Jesus of Nazareth must in some way conflate to that supernatural reality contemplated by the Platonists. John's language about Logos, the Word, as a preexisting reality was conflated with Jesus the individual very much because Jesus himself used terms like "life eternal." The transition from the language of idealism to the identification of Jesus with the Ideal was perhaps seen as an inescapable logical step, yet the Church was also confronted with the necessity to proclaim the undeniable reality of Jesus the human being. It led to that difficult language of the Creed produced at Nicaea.

But John's Gospel need not lead us into the philosophic direction of the Neo-Platonists. If we listen for the message of Jesus within John's terminology, we hear the distinctive message of Jesus and the biblical tradition from which his voice arises.

John MacQuarrie notes that John uses language that sounds much like that of Greek philosophy current in his cultural world—terms like *knowledge*, *truth*, and *light*. But, asks MacQuarrie, is knowledge here "in spite of the affinity with Greek thinking, as theoretical or speculative?" On the contrary, he says, John's usage of such terms "is to bring knowledge and truth from the spheres of the theoretical to the practical." For John, "Christ himself is the truth—not his discourses only, but primarily himself in his life and death and resurrection ... The Johannine conception of the Knowledge of God which is 'life eternal' is essentially like the concepts of knowledge and understanding which we found in the other biblical writers. It is a knowledge of the kind we call existential."[25]

Rudolf Bultmann says that for St. Paul, this experience of spiritual reality, "by detaching man from the world, makes him capable of fellowship in community." It is experienced as "new life," enabling man to be a new creature freed from his previous bondage in sin. It is also realized as the freedom to obey—to obey the call of Jesus and the Jewish tradition to live in service to others. The call is thus an imperative to obey the will of God as reflected in the ethical responsibilities inherited within the cultural tradition.[26]

But Bultmann argues that the call of Jesus as detailed in the New Testament is distinct from the demands of a "natural understanding of Being." For Bultmann, the kingdom of God of which Jesus speaks is "supernatural, superhistorical, that man can enter but not create in an historical sense."[27] Man is incapable of abandoning his "fallenness" by himself. He is freed of his anxiety only by the "saving act of God"—that is, the death and resurrection of Jesus as described in the New Testament.[28] Thus, for all the language of existentialism in his theology, Bultmann is ultimately a believer in supernatural realism. Only intervention by the saving act from beyond the natural world enables man to achieve authenticity, according to Bultmann.

But Jesus himself did not say to his followers that his upcoming death on the cross was the only means of salvation.

What he told them was that they must take up their own cross in this world by dying to the inauthentic way of being offered by "this world" and accept another way of living. His message was to live according to the Golden Rule, a message that his listeners knew had been current in their culture for centuries. The kingdom of God was always a possibility for humans to aspire to achieve on earth. It was and is the ever-present possibility of authenticity. Is it an ideal? Of course it is, but it is meaningful only in terms of human potential.

To be called by Jesus is to be called to a way of living that is, and can only be, of this world. For St. Paul, living in Christ is living out the values Jesus taught, but these must be lived out in an existence with the same bodily limitations for each individual as those faced by Jesus of Nazareth. It means moving from living by the normalized, "worldly" cultural standards that have dominated relationships across cultures and centuries, and to be reborn into relationships based on values that are called eternal or spiritual because they are ethical values that transcend the life of any one human. As these eternal values become incorporated into living out our corporeal lives, we say that "the spirit lives in us" because we attempt to live in accordance to those values.

To say that that the values espoused by Jesus were, and are, "of God," or that Jesus himself is "of God," is to acknowledge that these speak to our human condition in a profound way, but they apply to our human condition and arise from our human condition. They reflect values that address each of us in our finite, limited period of living but transcend those individual limitations and are thus universal and unlimited.

The followers of Jesus who experienced what we might describe as spiritual revelations—the "transfiguration" and encounters with a "resurrected" Jesus—reflect the powerful nature of their encounter with a person who so profoundly embodied this. Indeed, the ministry, sacrificial death, and "resurrection" of Jesus are a metaphor for the love of God, in the sense that they are a revelation of the nature of that which has made all life and made man for who he truly is.

CONCLUSION

Let us now circle back to our starting point: the Hebraic and Hellenistic traditions and their unwieldy conjoining in the Nicene Creed. The Hebraic tradition tells stories of human life. If some of these stories are apocryphal, they are nevertheless about lives as conditional as our own. These are lives of men and women who are as limited as our own in their duration and potential for knowledge. The Hellenistic tradition speaks to the capaciousness and potentiality of our minds, creations that transcend the limits of our individual lives, bring the world to our understanding, and speak of perfection and the ideal. They suggest that there are aspects of our essential nature that partake of the eternal, the ultimate reality, the very essence of truth.

The existentialists tell us that these traditions reveal who we are because they reflect fundamental aspects of our existence. We cannot abandon either without losing an understanding of ourselves. The Creed reflects each tradition in its linkage of the life of Jesus and the eternal ideals reflected by his life. The Creed is an effort to unite these in language that is of its own time and place, yet nevertheless it speaks to us. Our task must be to separate out the supernatural elements from the Creed so that we may mine what is true and authentic in what it says about Christianity and about Christianity and us.

NOTES

1   William Barrett, **Irrational Man** (Garden City, New York, 1962).
2   Barrett, 218–219.
3   Barrett, 221.
4   Barrett, 221.
5   Barrett, 223.
6   Barrett, 230–232.
7   Barrett, 235.
8   Barrett, 224.
9   Barrett, 224–226.
10 Barrett, 116.
11 Barrett, 237.
12 Barrett, 237.
13 John MacQuarrie, *An Existential Theology: A Comparison of Heidegger and Bultmann* (London: SCM Press, 1955). Questia. com, April 4, 2017.
14 MacQuarrie, 19.
15 MacQuarrie, 20.
16 MacQuarrie, 20.
17 MacQuarrie, 62.
18 MacQuarrie, 58.
19 MacQuarrie, 76.
20 MacQuarrie, 75.

21   MacQuarrie, 76.

22   MacQuarrie, 72–73.

23   MacQuarrie, 64.

24   Barrett, 143.

25   MacQuarrie, 66.

26   Rudolf Bultmann, *The Mythological Element in the Message of the New Testament and the Problem of its Re-Interpretation*, Part 2, p. 8 (www.religion-online, October 31, 2017).

27   Rudolf Bultmann, *Jesus and the Word of God,* Chapter 2, p. 10 (www.religion-online, October 31, 2017).

28   Bultmann, *The Mythological Element*, 11.

ABOUT THE AUTHOR

Robert High Baker holds a PhD in English from the University of Texas at Austin (1979). His dissertation was entitled "Aspects of Existential Phenomenology in the Works of Henry David Thoreau," and this focus in graduate school led to a lifetime of interest in existentialism as a hermeneutic approach that could be applied to many areas of study. Soon after graduation he left academia to enter the business world, but his interest in the humanities remained, including an ever-deepening interest in Christian theology.

Printed in the United States
By Bookmasters